Morning at the Beach

Buscher511@gmail.com

This book is dedicated
to children who love to read,
love sunshine,
love to watch pelicans,
love to hear the seagulls,
love to hunt seashells,
love to run on the sand
and to dip their toes in the surf.
Those children will love to go to the beach.

...Nancy Tancey Buscher

The sun climbs the horizon.
Rich gold rays spread about.
A new day is beginning.
Of that there is no doubt.

Palm trees, sway with little breeze,
and grasses on the dune.
You can hear them if you listen.
Their dry fronds click a tune.

The cool sea rushes forward.
The surf breaks on the shore.
A crab crawls out of hiding,
then two, then several more.

Wet shells glisten in the sun
as morning tide rolls in.
It stops for just a moment
and then rolls out again.

Sea foam gathers near the rocks
where waves come with a crash
that burst into the jetty
and water pellets flash.

Coquina wash upon the shore
and falter on the land.
They quickly take a nose dive
and burrow in the sand.

The swooping gulls call loudly
"Wake up. Let's start the day."
They spin and spiral higher,
then turn and fly away.

Out in the deeper water,
gray dolphins dive and dash.
Oh, you may see them jumping.
You will not hear them splash.

Pelicans fly overhead.
The hunt for food's begun.
Terns and cranes join gladly,
but Jays scold everyone.

Grasses wave upon the shore,
the sun warms everyone,
wake up, wake up, it seems to say,
a new day has begun.

Did You Know?

Our sun is a star.

Our sun is the largest object in our solar system.

The sun looks yellow, but it's actually white.

It is dangerous to look directly at the sun.

There are over 2,500 kinds of palm trees.

The Quindio wax palm is the tallest and can grow up to 197'.

South Carolina is known as the Palmetto State.

Palmetto logs were used to build Fort Moultry,
near Charleston, South Carolina, around the time of
the Revolutionary War because cannonballs
bounced off tem.

What crab is pictured on page 8?

This crab begins as an egg, goes to a zoea, then a megalopa,
then a juvenile, to an adult who lay eggs and life begins again.

Which of the two shells on page 11 is a Cockle Shell?

Slipper shells look like a tiny person's slipper.

Turkey Wing looks like its name.

Sanibel Island, Florida, is said to be one of the 10 best beaches for shell hunting.

A jetty is a structure that goes out into water. The Venice jetty was constructed in 1937.

Venice has a north jetty and a south jetty. It's fun to watch for manatee and dolphin.

If you take or buy food at the jetty, birds may come begging. And watch for pelicans.

Coquina are tiny clams found along sea coasts worldwide.

Coquina are very colorful.

Coquina measure up to 1" long.

Coquina are bivalve, so when open they remind you of butterfles.

Gulls are often confused with terns.

Gulls have broad wings and tern's wings are pointed.

Gulls have hooked bills and terns have pointed bills.

Gulls are bigger than terns.

Gulls float on the water for prey, terns dive into the water.

Does a dolphin have a nose? No, it has a blow hole like a whale.

Dolphins and whales are related to hippos. Just like a manatee is related to elephants.

A pelican's pouch is called a gular.

American pelicans plunge-dive for fish. They hit feet first and scoop fish into their pouch.

Before dusk a few pelicans will fly along the shore and are joined by others forming a line or V before they roost for the night.

Grasses at the beach anchor the sand so the wind doesn't blow it all away.

Many dune grasses prevent the loss of water and reflect drying sunlight.

Dune grasses are also habitat for birds, lizards and rabbits to name a few.

———————————————————

Hardcover

At the Beach
Brandon Grows a Vine
Emma's Dilemma

Paperback

Kaleidoscope of Children's Poems-2
Lucky Dog Diner

Paperback Chapter Books
Elfwood, the Shiny Silver Steam Engine
Elfwood, the Great Pumpkin Plot

MacKenzie says, Cool Kids Read

Emma's Dilemma was written by Nancy Tancey Buscher and illustrated by Lori Loveberry George.

You can get it on Amazon or contact the writer. Ask Nancy to autograph it for you.

My neighbor, Mrs. Tuttlehead, gave me a plant. It was pretty little when she gave it to me.

I guess I did a good job taking care of it. It sure isn't little any more.

Brandon Grows a Vine was written by Nancy Tancey Buscher and illustrated by Lori Loveberry George.

If you like plants and like to see things grow, you'll want to read my book.

You can get it on Amazon or contact the writer. Ask Nancy to autograph it for you.

The poem *Fence Cats* was the inspiration for *The Christmas Cat-Astrophe,* the musical first produced for Piccolo- Spoleto, Charleston, South Carolina's annual cultural festival. It was the only children's play that year.
Play and lyrics by Nancy Buscher, music by Virginia Neill.

Kaleidoscope of Children's Poems - 2 is a sampling of different poetic styles. It

---

Fancy and Buster go to the Grand Opening of the *Lucky Dog Diner*. Buster is hungry, but Fancy tells him they have to wait till after the Parade of Stars. Sandwiches have been named for these special canine guests. But can Buster wait?

<u>COMING SOON</u>

Watch for New Books
By
Nancy Tancey Buscher

(Ages 3-5)
Maybe Crybaby
Wiggly Giggly Girls

(Ages 7-9)
Elfwood, The Great Pumpkin Plot
Collection of Short Stories

(Ages 7-9)
Flit Flutter Fly
Collection of Short Stories